Infer

Maggie Jones is author of *Trying to Have a Baby*, *Everything you Need to Know About Adoption*, *Now or Never*, *The First 12 Months*, *Play and Learn* and *Safety and Your Child*. She also writes for *Best*, *Parents*, the *Sunday Times*, *Observer* and the *Independent*. Maggie is married with three small children.

Infertility

MODERN TREATMENTS AND THE ISSUES THEY RAISE

MAGGIE JONES

PIATKUS

© 1991 Maggie Jones
First published in 1989 as *A Child by Any Means*

This revised and updated edition
published in 1991 by Judy Piatkus
(Publishers) Limited, 5 Windmill Street,
London W1P 1HF

British Library Cataloguing in Publication Data

Jones, Maggie, *1953* –
   Infertility: modern treatments and the issues they raise.
   1. Man. Infertility. Therapy
   I. Title
   616.69206

   ISBN 0 – 7499 – 1031 – 3

Edited by Maggie Daykin
Designed by Sue Ryall

Typeset by Action Typesetting Limited, Gloucester
Printed and bound in Great Britain by
Mackays of Chatham PLC

Contents

Acknowledgements

We would like to thank Professor R. G. Edwards for granting us permission to reproduce the diagram on page 22 from the book *Conception in the Human Female* published by Academic Press, and Thorsons Publishing Group Limited for the diagram on page 16 from the book *Now or Never* by Bostock and Jones, 1987.

Introduction

Many books have been published on the subject of infertility, the new techniques which may overcome it, and the ethical issues involved, but none have looked closely into how the couples concerned feel, what solutions they have come to, or how they feel towards the children born as a result of new technology, especially those who are not their genetic offspring. There are further questions too. Why do most people want children? What are the problems faced by the infertile? What are the new options available to them? How do they feel about these options? How will they adapt to a new kind of parenthood? What are children born through IVF, through embryo, sperm and egg donation, going to feel? What can be done to protect their interests? What rights do they have to learn about their origins and about their biological parents? Will the new technologies give birth to families that are no different to conventional ones or will we be creating new kinds of stepfamilies, with the sort of problems many of these now face?

Sometimes this book may appear to raise more questions than answers, because I believe the best decisions about new fertility treatment will only come through listening to the voices of those who have experienced it or are affected by it – or will be in the future – the infertile, their families, and the children they may ultimately be helped to bear.

Whether you are 'infertile' and, in trying to conceive, need information on all the options and implications, or simply want to be better informed on this major – many would say 'vital' – issue of our time, I hope this book will be a helpful introduction to these complex issues.

MIRACLES OF MODERN SCIENCE

Through the various combinations of techniques for obtaining eggs and sperm and for fertilising and reimplanting them, there are now at least 16 different ways to have a child.

- A child can be conceived naturally or through artificial insemination or through in vitro fertilisation (IVF).
- The eggs can come from the mother or from a donor, the sperm from the father or a donor, or both can come from a donor.
- The baby can be carried in the womb of a surrogate mother, who also provided the egg, or a host mother, who carries a child which is not genetically hers.
- A child can also be conceived posthumously through frozen eggs, sperm or embryos.

A chart detailing these various combinations appears in Chapter 4, where the techniques are fully explained. These new scientific techniques which have enabled infertile couples to achieve their dream have brought with them a host of other developments that a few years ago would have been dismissed as science fiction but have now become reality:

- A grandmother bore and gave birth to her daughter's triplets.
- Twin embryos were stored deep frozen for months and then born 18 months apart.
- Babies born prematurely at 22 weeks have survived, some without handicap.
- Women who have passed the menopause are being helped to conceive and give birth.

Indeed, science has moved so fast that medical opinion, popular opinion and the law have hardly been able to keep pace, giving rise to practical, social, emotional and ethical problems.

REACTIONS

In 1990, the British government passed the Human Fertilisation and Embryology Act which finally set up a legal framework to cover the new treatments for infertility, especially IVF (in vitro fertilisation) and treatments involving donated eggs, sperm and embryos. The new legislation followed on from the recommendations of the Warnock Committee. This was set up in 1982, headed by Dame Mary Warnock, to look into the practical and ethical problems raised by new treatments for infertility. The subsequent report, published in 1984, provided a basis for legislation and, after further wide consultation, the government published its White Paper on Human Fertilisation and Embryology, in December 1987.

The new legislation clears up a number of issues which till then had been unclear. The legislation will finally ensure that children born in the UK following the donation of sperm, eggs or embryos will be the legitimate children of the family into which they are born. Children born from sperm and eggs donated by the future parents but carried by a surrogate mother will be the legitimate children of the genetic parents if the surrogate mother agrees, and will not have to go through formal adoption proceedings. The Human Fertilisation and Embryology Authority will hold information on donors, and include the name and date of birth of the child and a reference number for the donor. All adults over the age of 18 will have the right to find out whether they were born through sperm, egg or embryo donation and, if so, have access to information about the donor.

Surrogacy arrangements, covered by the Surrogacy Arrangements Act 1985, were not altered by the new legislation; a clause stating that 'no surrogacy arrangement is enforceable by or against any of the persons making it' has been added. Some medical centres have announced that they intend to arrange and carry out surrogate pregnancies for their patients, though these cannot be enforced in law and no money can change hands. The potential parents have to take the risk that the surrogate mother might not give up the baby at birth.

The Warnock report concluded that *certain infertility treatments such as IVF and those involving donated eggs, sperm and embryos should be permitted, subject to statutory control by an independent body. The report also made recommendations on surrogate motherhood (commercial surrogacy should be made illegal and surrogacy was to be discouraged), the storage and disposal of human embryos, eggs and sperm, the status of children born after embryos, egg or sperm donation and the development of infertility services generally, including counselling.*

Warnock recommended that a Statutory Licensing Authority be set up to inspect and control centres in which the new infertility treatments and embryo research might be carried out. This Authority should be 'independent of Government, health authorities and research institutions' and not made up entirely by doctors and similar professionals. In 1985 the Royal College of Obstetricians and Gynaecologists and the Medical Research Council set up a Voluntary Licensing Authority (VLA) along these lines to act as a watchdog in the meantime. The VLA, despite having no 'teeth', nonetheless proved successful in regulating treatments at the infertility centres known to and registered with them, for example setting an upper limit to the numbers of embryos or eggs to be transferred in IVF or GIFT treatments. Following the decision to set up a statutory licensing authority in the debate on the embryo bill, the VLA changed its name to the Interim Licensing Authority, and it will be replaced by the Human Fertilisation and Embryology Authority in August 1991.

The HFEA will grant licences for: infertility treatments involving the creation of embryos in vitro; using donated eggs, sperm or embryos; the storage of eggs, sperm and embryos; and for embryo research. Embryo research will be allowed only for purposes laid down in the new legislation (see page 98).

The Department of Health will draw up regulations to cover for such questions as the exact information on donors which can be revealed to children seeking information about their origins, the circumstances in which eggs, sperm or embryos can be stored for longer than the upper limit fixed in the Act, and the circumstances in which embryos can be kept or used.

Surrogate motherhood has caused dilemmas on a world-wide scale. In Australia, the committees which considered aspects of assisted reproduction stopped short of recommending the actual criminalisaton of surrogate motherhood, feeling that if surrogate contracts were not recognised in law and advertising to recruit surrogate mothers were illegal this would be enough to discourage it. Only in Canada did the Ontario Law Reform Commission suggest that surrogate contracts be recognised, and be made enforceable, even if this meant seizing the child from the surrogate mother. The Commission felt that this would be in the best interests of the child, and that the surrogate mother would know the score in advance. However, this has not passed into law.

LEADING ISSUES

The new fertility treatments have led to much debate, inside parliament and out, about the nature of human life, the right of a couple to have a child, and the rights of children born through new fertility techniques. One of the most emotive issues to be raised universally, following the development of IVF, was the question of the rights of the embryos created outside the human body and the use of such embryos for research; research which is now allowed for up to 14 days from fertilisation. Despite the go-ahead to research given by MPs in a surprisingly large majority – 364 MPs in favour and only 193 against, a majority of 171 – opposition has not been silenced and the debate goes on.

The debate about the provision of modern infertility treatments goes on too. Those who have personally suffered the tragic human consequences of being unable to have a child strongly protest their right to attempt to overcome their infertility with the new techniques available. Indeed, not only the majority of people who have experienced problems in conceiving, but also the majority of the general public, would support most forms of assisted reproduction, but there is fundamental opposition to either the principle or the various techniques available. The main arguments against assisted reproduction are:

- **That it is not natural.** People who support this view often say that it is not right to over-ride God or nature in this matter, that a couple or individual should be reconciled to their childlessness and find other ways of fulfilment. The counter argument is that most modern medical treatment could be viewed as 'unnatural' and that to reject it as such is falling into the extremism showed by religious groups such as Christian Scientists and Jehovah's Witnesses who will not even allow a dying relative a blood transfusion.

- **That infertility is not a disease.** Though infertility may not strictly be a disease, it is often the result of a disease, such as diabetes or a sexually transmitted infection in the man, or a pelvic infection, past pelvic surgery, endometriosis or disease of the ovaries in a woman. The problem may be a malfunction of the hormonal system which, if not considered a disease, must be a disorder. Infertility is a fundamental malfunctioning of the human body and as such deserves medical treatment.

- **Having children is a luxury.** This argument is that even if infertility is a disease or disorder, it does not actually threaten the sufferer's life or continued existence, and therefore is not a priority for treatment. Having children is considered to be a luxury rather than to be an essential part of living.

  The opposite view is that reproducing himself is biologically the main purpose of man's existence. Illnesses which occur in later life, when a man has had his children, are unimportant in biological terms because they do not affect his ability to reproduce himself. Therefore it could be argued that they are less, not more, deserving of treatment.

- **Infertility treatment involves unacceptable practices.** Some argue that while straightforward treatments of infertility, such as repairing diseased tubes or giving drugs which do not have harmful side-effects might be acceptable, treatments which involve the donation or storing of sperm, eggs and embryos or which call for the participation of third parties such as surrogate mothers are not.

  The Catholic Church also argues that procedures

involving collection of sperm by masturbation are unacceptable. *Humanae Vitae,* Pope Paul VI's famous encyclical, issued in 1968, came out against the use of 'artificial' birth control methods by practising Catholics, and said quite clearly that the Church would not permit the separation or exclusion of the 'procreative intention or of the conjugal relationship.' Previously Pius XII wrote: 'To reduce the shared life of a married couple and the act of married love to a mere organic activity for transmitting semen would be like turning the domestic home, the sanctuary of the family, into a biological laboratory.' This view clearly expresses the disquiet which many Catholics, and others, feel about assisted reproduction. More recently, the Catholic Church has reiterated its opposition to IVF and other new reproductive techniques. Against this view, many argue that masturbation is a natural sexual outlet and if the child is born of a loving relationship, masturbation for the purpose of creating a child cannot be wrong.

- **Many treatments involve 'genealogical bewilderment' for the child.** This is one of the strongest arguments against techniques which separate genetic and social parenthood. However, for centuries children have been adopted, brought up by step-parents and conceived outside wedlock, and rising divorce and remarriage rates mean that an increasing number of children live with one parent who is not their natural parent and step- or half-brothers and sisters. Children conceived through assisted reproduction techniques and having different genetic and social parents would probably not add greatly to those numbers.

  Whether it is fair to specifically create children for such a situation is more difficult to answer although the evidence from children born through artificial insemination by donor is that while it might cause them some problems, few would prefer not to exist.

- **Why put such effort into creating a child when many children still wait to be adopted?** This is a valid question but, as fully discussed in Chapter 1 many people do want their own child – or a child as close to being their own as possible – and many women want to experience pregnancy, childbirth and breastfeeding. Also, many people are not considered suitable to adopt because of their age, previous divorce, race or other factors over which they have no control. Others do not feel able to cope with the demands made by children who may have had past unhappy experiences or who have severe disabilities. Others may not pass adoption screening procedures for reasons which are never divulged to them . . . often it may simply be that the social workers who assessed the couple do not like them or consider they would not make suitable parents for reasons which may be hard to qualify.

Most people adopt because they are unable to have their own children, not because they specifically want to bring up other children. It seems reasonable that many people might want to try every possibility of having a child which is their own, or at least of their partner's before thinking of adoption.

- **Assisted reproduction inevitably results in some experimentation on embryos.** Some assisted reproduction treatments such as IVF will involve the sacrifice of some embryos which cannot be used for implantation either because they seem to be developing less well than others, or because too many embryos have grown successfully. Embryos also have to be examined to check that they are normal and this could be considered as 'experimentation'. For those who find the concept of experimenting on embryos abhorrent, IVF and many other treatments will not be acceptable.

However, as the new legislation recognises, new fertility treatments are here to stay. Research on embryos into the nature of genetic disease will continue, and many more children will be born through these medical advances who would not otherwise have existed. These children, perhaps the most deeply concerned with the new laws, are the only ones who have not had a voice. What will they say about these new technologies? How will they feel about the donors of the eggs or sperm from which they grew? And the fate of the spare embryos conceived with them? And the new kinds of families in which they will live? In the meantime, the children who have already been brought up by non-genetic parents (through adoption, divorce and remarriage and AID) have many lessons to teach us, as will be clear from reading Chapter 7.

Infertility

1

Why we want children

In recent years the number of articles on couples' struggles to overcome their infertility have grown apace. More than ever, it seems, we want to have children. After a brief period in the 1960s and 70s when a vocal minority of couples sought freedom from the ties and responsibilities of family life, and stated concern about the future of our overpopulated planet, the family is back in fashion. Not only do some politicians sing the virtues of the family unit, not always for altruistic reasons, but we are seeing a new interest in children as part of our consumer culture, with the growth of designer toys, baby equipment and babywear. Even a number of recent Hollywood epics have given the star role to baby. Legislation enacted in the 70s to enable women to take maternity leave and return to their jobs, has made it easier for women to combine motherhood *and* a career.

Why do so many of us want children so much? Is it the age-old biological instinct which prevails? Or is a baby just another desirable possession – like a house, car, new kitchen – even the ultimate status symbol?

Those who *don't* want children – at least not until they have achieved all their other goals – often see motherhood as so low in status and children so demanding and disrupting to an ordered lifestyle that they fail to understand what reasons there could be for wanting children. So, there is a dual attitude to motherhood: on the one hand it is seen in a romantic way as a woman's vocation and true role in life, and on the other as a boring, repetitive task peripheral to career success or social advancement. Reluctance to take on such a commitment may also be influenced by the fact that so many marriages break down, that there are many unwanted pregnancies and that physical and sexual child abuse is rising. Such considerations tend to blind some people to the hope, joys and pleasures also involved in having children.

In particular, some people may find it hard to understand the desperation of those who find themselves unable to have children, and wonder why they are prepared, with or without the help of new medical technology, to go to extraordinary lengths to have a child they can call their own. They may even perceive the infertile as selfish, or neurotic people, who should accept their situation and make the best of it, or even be grateful that they are not burdened with children and can be 'childfree'.

Yet this question of wanting or not wanting children is a very recent one. Only in the present century has there been any real choice for the great majority of people.

THE OLD FAMILY ORDER

In the past, sexual liaisons led almost inevitably to the birth of children and social structures were created to prevent sexual relationships outside of a stable marriage bond, and to guarantee that the children a man brought up were his. Any children born to the marriage were assumed to be the genetic descendents of their parents, the children of their own flesh and blood. When relationships did occur outside of marriage, the children of such unions were branded illegitimate and did not enjoy the rights of children conceived within a marriage.

THE FAMILY TODAY

Even today, when Western societies accept the idea of an equal marriage partnership, children are still considered for the most part the property of their parents, who can control almost every aspect of their lives. Only under extreme circumstances, when their life or safety is held to be at stake, can children be removed from their parents or extended families and taken into care.

Children of a marriage are still assumed to be the genetic offspring of their parents, and if they are not, it is often kept secret. As recounted in myth and literature from earliest times, where a child is not the blood relation of both parents, there may be trouble: stepchildren persecuted by stepmothers or stepfathers, a changeling taking the place of a couple's natural child and causing problems in the family, adopted children who turn out badly in one way or another. These stories, buried deep in our consciousness, continue to influence our ideas and create the feeling that only our own biological or blood children will truly satisfy us.

Parents and grandparents are delighted when their children or grandchildren inherit clearly recognisable characteristics from them. It gives them a sense of immortality – that something of them is going on into the future and will endure after their death. In having children we fulfil our biological purpose, and although few people today would say this was the most important reason for their existence, at some deep level there still seems a recognition that this is the case.

In many societies adoption has always existed to care for orphaned children and to provide offspring for those unable to have their own. Adoption is normally recognised through a formal declaration that this child will be treated 'as if' he or she were the natural child of the family, whether this is recognised in law or not. However, some family members can not forget the absence of the blood tie, and the child may be made very aware of this, or have to prove his gratitude and loyalty over the years.

DEVELOPMENT OF CONTRACEPTION

In modern times family foundations have been rocked by a rapid series of changes, all based on the development of technologies which, for the first time in human history, enable men and women to effectively separate sexual experience from reproduction. The first major breakthrough was the development of modern methods of contraception – although contraception has existed in various forms for centuries. These were mainly spermicidal preparations inserted into the woman's vagina – pessaries made out of crocodile-dung were reported in ancient Egypt – or condoms such as those made of sheep's gut popularised by Casanova in the eighteenth century. In the nineteenth century the use of home-made vaginal sponges and withdrawal were recommended, and by the end of the century early caps to cover the cervix and spermicidal pessaries were developed.

However, these contraceptives were not very effective, not widely available and, indeed, not socially approved of. Condoms were used more to prevent the passing on of sexually transmitted diseases than to prevent pregnancies. Only in the mid-twentieth century were more effective contraceptive methods made available to ordinary men and women.

THE SEXUAL REVOLUTION

In the early 1960s came the real breakthroughs: the contraceptive Pill, IUDs suitable for childless women, and quick, safe methods of both male and female sterilisation. These much safer methods of contraception revolutionised social attitudes towards sex and its expression. The 'permissive society' made possible sexual relationships with no commitment on either side to form a permanent liaison and have a family. By the late 1960s abortion had been made legal on both medical and social grounds, divorce law was reformed to enable couples to split up more easily and remove the concept of 'guilty' and 'innocent' parties and family planning clinics had opened their doors to unmarried people seeking contraceptive advice and supplies.

The sexual revolution was on the whole greeted as not a bad thing, freeing men and women to find greater happiness, greater sexual fulfilment and, for women especially, making it possible to compete on more equal terms with men in the workplace and exercise personal control over whether or when to have children.

However, this new freedom was not without its dark side. Many women found that without the protection of marriage and the threat of pregnancy, men used them for sexual fulfilment without providing the security they needed for a happy relationship. Even 'effective' contraception was not without its side-effects and risks – which the woman usually had to bear – and there were occasions when it failed and an unwanted pregnancy resulted. Few women have an abortion without considerable feelings of sadness and guilt and many underwent the experience without the support of their partner who had entered the relationship with no intention of a lasting commitment.

THE NEW WOMAN

Perhaps the most significant effect of the separation of sexuality from reproduction has been the freeing of many women from purely domestic responsibilities. During the two world wars women proved that they could work outside the home and the numbers of women in employment outside the home has increased steadily. Women have also achieved higher and higher offices. The numbers of women doctors, politicians, lawyers and executives continue to rise, though many say too slowly.

However, pressures are still brought to bear on women through laws, religion and social structures which assume that women will give birth to the children on whom society depends, and take the central role in bringing them up. Because it is assumed that women will have children, some employers are still reluctant to take women on. Also, although most working women now have the statutory right to paid maternity leave, it is not unusual for firms to pass them over for promotion or in other ways curtail their career after they have had a baby. In particular, women who can no longer work some shifts or stay late at the office because they have a young family may find it difficult to get promotion or well-paid jobs. This may discourage some ambitious women from having families, but it probably also makes more women give up work to become full-time mothers because such pressures make it not worth trying to succeed at both. A large number of women, however, do not really have a choice; financial necessity obliges them to take whatever work they can find.

For these various reasons family size has continued to fall, and there has been an increasing trend for many women to delay childbearing and have fewer children later in life. In the UK, the number of first babies born to mothers who have been married for between 10 and 14 years has doubled over the last ten years, and births to mothers aged 30 to 39 had increased from nearly 112,000 in 1974 out of 640,000 live births to 165,500 out of 637,000 live births in 1984.

As women in many countries have become less financially dependent on their husbands and have found alternative sources of satisfaction to being simply wives and mothers, divorce rates also have soared. One in three marriages is now expected to end in divorce. Remarriage is the norm, adding an increasing number of step-families and reconstituted families to the rising numbers of single-parent families left in the wake of divorce. These, together with dual-earning families with and without children, now outnumber the number of 'traditional' families with wage- or salary-earning father, stay-at-home mother and children. Also, as unemployment rises, increasing numbers of families have no wage-earner or have working wives and stay-at-home husbands.

HOMOSEXUALITY AND FAMILY LIFE

Along with changing attitudes to sexuality during the 1960s came a change in society's attitude to homosexuality. Legal reform meant that homosexual acts between consenting adults over 21 was no longer a crime, and increasing numbers of homosexual men and women chose to openly declare their sexual orientation and to live with their partner in a long-term relationship. Some men divorced their wives but kept up contact with their children; some lived with male partners *and* cared for the children of their previous marriage. Many lesbian women decided that they wanted to raise children, sometimes conceiving a child with a male friend sympathetic to their position or resorting to artificial insemination. Lesbian groups instructed women in 'self-insemination', a technique that has gone out of fashion since the AIDS epidemic started as many groups used homosexual men as sperm donors. Lesbian women may find a sympathetic doctor who will provide them with artificial insemination on the NHS or may be able to use a private clinic. (See also Chapter 4.)

TO HAVE OR HAVE NOT

As sexuality has been slowly and irresistibly separated from its consequence of producing children, many couples have increasingly given thought to whether they really want to have children or why they want to have children. The question, 'Why children?' is asked more and more today – indeed, it only has relevance now that such a choice, not to have children, is possible. There are many reasons why some find it hard to understand why most people choose to have children: for example, the expense, the disruption of careers and lifestyles, the exhaustion felt by many parents and the low status given to stay-at-home mothers. Some people also fear that their relationship with their partner will not only alter but actually suffer when children enter the picture. Women may also fear or simply wish to avoid the damage done to their bodies by pregnancy and childbirth in a culture which portrays only the very young and slim as being sexually desirable.

Even so, those who choose not to have children are still in a minority. Indeed, the separation of sexuality from reproduction may not be as complete as we like to think.

Many people find great difficulty in using contraception effectively, even if the consequences of having a baby are very undesirable. Studies have shown that a majority of young people do not use contraception the first time they have sexual intercourse and that a large number do not use effective contraception at all. This is not merely due to the difficulty in some countries or embarrassment of obtaining contraception, or even the conviction that 'It won't happen to me'. Many people have real difficulties in planning in a rational way for an irrational event. Others find the idea of risking pregnancy in itself exciting; or perhaps they would like a child, even if the circumstances are inappropriate.

Whatever the reasons, many pregnancies remain unplanned. The Family Planning Association estimates that there are about 200,000 unwanted pregnancies in Britain every year, over half of which end in abortion. The women who have unwanted pregnancies are no different from others. A study carried out in the United States by Kristen Luker, *Taking Chances: Abortion and the Decision Not to Contracept*, of young women who were having repeat abortions found that the only way in which these women differed from their peers was that they had been unlucky. However, theories that women who have repeat abortions have some underlying desire to get pregnant but then cannot go through with it may be true for a very few.

For many young people, the idea of pregnancy seems so horrific and so remote that they do not believe that it can happen to them. They certainly do not have sexual relationships out of an underlying need to have a baby.

Natural selection may have made sexuality pleasurable in order to lure the human race into reproducing itself, and most people – especially women – find babies and young children delightful and appealing, but they are also often afraid of them. The fact that in our society many people have never held a baby or seen one breastfed until they have their own makes most people afraid of handling infants because they do not know how to deal with them. In the small families of today, most people will have been too young to remember the birth of their younger brothers and sisters, and will have had no part in helping to bring them up.

The idea of having children seems frightening because most couples have no idea what to expect. So although parental instincts do exist, they seem to be outweighed today by fears of parental inadequacy. This has led to a proliferation of babycare books giving detailed information about how to change nappies, how to feed babies, how to bath them, dress them and help them sleep.

So is there such a thing as a 'maternal instinct'? It seems clear that women need to learn how to be mothers, whether from their own mothers, or from books and health professionals. Most aspects of motherhood do not come 'naturally', though the desire to do what is right for the baby does.

Mothers – and babies – have always been victims of medical and other advice, which has suggested such practices as not putting the baby to the breast till the milk comes in (this led to many maternal deaths from 'milk fever' in seventeenth century Europe); feeding on a four-hourly rota and leaving the baby to cry in between; bottle- rather than breastfeeding, or feeding the baby solid foods from an early age. Each generation of mothers has had to find her way through a mass of conflicting advice and misinformation; only the lucky ones, confident in their own instincts, have had the confidence to put such advice aside.

Some writers such as Elizabeth Badinter in her historical review, *The Myth of Motherhood*, have denied the existence of maternal instincts altogether, and found plenty of evidence to support this view, such as mothers who put their babies out to wet-nurses and showed no signs of grief when they died. However, other letters and books from this period show how much mothers did grieve their dead children and how much joy they found in the ones who thrived and grew. In every generation there will be a mixture of 'good' and 'bad' mothers. The support that society gives to mothers and families generally will have a lot to do with how well women cope with the pressures of motherhood.

REWARDS OF PARENTHOOD

Having children probably represents the most significant and traumatic experience a person ever experiences, apart from birth itself and death, neither of which we can have any memories of. In a way it forms the final separation from one's own childhood. People see themselves primarily as the children of their parents until, suddenly, they are parents in their turn.

Now they and their children are the immediate family. For the first time they are no longer expected to 'go home' for Christmas; home is now where the young children are.

In the immediate period after the birth, most parents find themselves the focus of praise and congratulations. Many mothers, in particular, find the few days after the birth an intensely rewarding time. They are made a tremendous fuss of by hospital staff, by relatives and friends, and by colleagues from work. If their working life has not given them any sense of reward and achievement, some mothers may even have more babies because they feel this is the only experience through which they have been acknowledged to have done something important.

Young, single women who get pregnant might have equally complex reasons for doing so. They may have had a child to 'trap a man into marriage', or to force parents and others to acknowledge a relationship, to fill up time if they and their partner are unemployed or unable to find worthwhile jobs, even to gain financial support or a home if local authorities give priority to single mothers or couples with children.

One young woman acknowledged that she had 'got herself pregnant' because it was proof to herself and her boyfriend that something important had happened between them. 'He said that just because we slept together didn't mean that the relationship was important to him. He kept denying that it meant something. So I stopped taking the Pill and got pregnant nearly straightaway. I thought, now he won't ever be able to forget me. He won't be able to pretend to our friends or his family that there wasn't really anything going on between us.'

On the positive side, in the case of many couples *both* partners want to have a child, as a physical bond between them, a living proof of their loving relationship. As one man put it, 'If we don't have a child there will be nothing to show that we were together or loved one another. If we have a child, somehow we will be joined forever.'

Couples often say they want a child because the child will be someone for them to love, who will also give them love in return. Some people want children to relive their happy childhood experiences, or sometimes to make up for the lack of them.

Sometimes people see children as important in forming a blood link between their families. 'Before, it was just "his family" and "my family". Now we have the children, we are all related to one another.'

MOTHERHOOD

There is no doubt that many women profoundly enjoy the experience of pregnancy, childbirth and motherhood. Some enjoy it so much that they have several children, in an age where having two is considered the norm and anything above this rather exceptional. Many women find being pregnant exciting and rewarding, despite physical discomforts such as morning sickness or the heaviness of late pregnancy. One mother said:

'I love my body when I'm pregnant. It seems round, full, complete somehow. I find that I am emotionally on an even keel throughout; no more pre-menstrual depressions and upsets. I love the sensation of a baby moving. I love the feeling that I am never alone, yet at the same time I am my own person. If I could always be five months pregnant, life would be bliss.'

Childbirth can be a woman's greatest experience despite the pain which is often emphasised to the exclusion of almost all else. Breastfeeding, too, can be a powerful physical experience and an emotional bond which provides immense rewards. Again, a mother talks of her feelings about these experiences:

'It's such a tremendous thing, you can't imagine what life will be like when it's all behind you. Nowadays we are conditioned to the idea that it's sexual intercourse which is all important, and that we mustn't be without it. Yet I've found pregnancy, childbirth and breastfeeding just as pleasurable as sex. When I weaned my last baby it was terrible; as if someone said, well that's it, you'll never have sex again.'

Of course, the satisfaction that children bring are not only felt on a physical or emotional level. In many developing countries people want children also because they are their wealth – especially sons – and will bring money into the family to help their parents in old age. Even though that does not really apply in most developed countries where there is state provision for the elderly, people are often still afraid of how they will fare in old age if they have no children. Needs are by no means only financial, either. In old age childless couples may feel alone and isolated, with no children or grandchildren to visit them or keep them in touch with the world. They may have good friends and neighbours, but it is not the same:

'There isn't anyone I feel I can ask to help me. If I ask the neighbours to do something for me, I feel that I have to do something back, like taking their cat in when they're late home and giving her supper, or giving them apples from the garden. It's only family you can ask things as of right, and now I have no family. If something happened to me, there would be no-one for them to ring, no-one to come to the bedside. Without family, who will care?'

People have always looked to their children for security in their old age, and though nowadays not all children are prepared to take on the problems of elderly parents, many do. At any rate, children are people to look after your affairs if you become less able to look after them yourself and people to turn to in a crisis, to leave your possessions to, to organise your funeral.

LOVED AND LOVING

People also want children because of a natural and powerful need to give and receive love. In our society we tend to have only a few truly intimate relationships, often restricted to the immediate family. If a couple have no children, they may have only one another to love, and can seem too great a burden to put on one another.

Children both need and give a great deal of physical affection, fulfilling the parents' need to touch and hold as well as their own. A happy household with children in it is full of noise, warmth, activity, hugs and kisses. Caring for their children gives parents a sense of warmth and security; making someone else feel safe makes us feel safe too. As one mother recalls, 'I never felt so happy as when they were small and I would tuck them into bed in the evening. I could make everything all right for them, and that made me feel that everything else in the world was right, too.'

Children also provide so much work and activity that there is little time for parents to wonder what the purpose of their lives is. The children need them; that is enough. Festivals like Christmas or birthdays take on a new meaning because they are done for the children. The children's response to them makes them magic, and we recall our own feelings in childhood before we became aware of the commercialisation of such holidays.

WANTING TOO MUCH

People who have had a happy childhood may want to relive the same pleasures with their children. People whose childhoods have not been happy may also want children so that they can create the happy childhood that they were denied. This may seem very important as a means to heal the wounds of the past. Yet sometimes these parents may focus so much on making their children happy that they see their children too much as a route to their own fulfilment. This can poison parent-child relationships and make things go badly wrong.

Parents who see children as extensions of themselves and try to make their children achieve the goals they wanted to achieve – but often failed or lacked the opportunity to pursue – seldom achieve the satisfaction they seek and may instead alienate their children. Children whose parents focus too much on what they achieve may feel that they are not loved for themselves, only for what they can do. The insecurity created may make the child reject his work or behave badly in order to test whether his parents will still love him nonetheless.

Some people who have had a child or children after years of infertility, or with the help of new fertility techniques, view their children as even more important to them, and find it harder to let go of them when they reach adolescence. There is some evidence that this is true of adopted children (see Chapter 4). There is a danger that in wanting so much to have a 'baby', one forgets the child and then the adult the baby becomes. In the words of one woman who had test-tube twins at the fourth attempt, 'The fertility treatment is so demanding that you lose all sight of what it's for. I found myself suddenly asking, what if I don't even like parenthood at the end of all this?'

Let this woman's comment lead us into the next chapter, which looks at the causes and treatment of infertility, and the emotions and experience of those who are infertile but most certainly do want children.

2

Infertility: causes, tests and treatments

Infertility is usually defined as the inability of a couple to conceive a child after a year of regular sexual intercourse. In fact, many couples who are 'infertile' by this definition will conceive eventually – either naturally or following infertility treatment. Infertility is a widespread problem – as many as one in six couples will consult their doctor because they are worried about not having conceived. Today, infertility may seem even harder to bear by a generation accustomed to using contraception, planning births – almost to the month – and having more choices and more control over their lives.

HOW CONCEPTION OCCURS

Human conception is a miraculous and complex event, and what is surprising is perhaps that pregnancy occurs so often, rather than that it sometimes fails. A human egg is released every month from a woman's ovary under the influence of a complex cycle of hormones released by the pituitary gland and the hypothalamus. The egg is swept into the fallopian tubes by the delicate projections (the fimbriae) at the end of the tubes, where it is normally fertilised by the man's sperm. The fertilised egg then moves down the tube and, aided by the tiny hair-like cilia which line the tube, enter the womb. The embryo

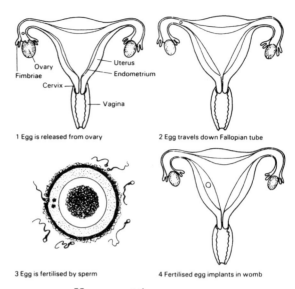

1 Egg is released from ovary

2 Egg travels down Fallopian tube

3 Egg is fertilised by sperm

4 Fertilised egg implants in womb

How conception occurs

must implant into the lining of the womb (the endometrium) where it starts to produce hormones which will stimulate its growth. The body in the ovary, the corpus luteum, from which the egg was released, must produce enough of the hormone progesterone to sustain the pregnancy until, after the first three months, the placenta takes over. The woman's womb must be structurally sound and capable of expanding to contain the growing foetus and the cervix strong enough to hold the baby in until it is ready to be born.

It is estimated that it takes a fertile couple having regular sexual intercourse an average of six months to conceive. At any stage, something can go wrong and a pregnancy will not result:

- Sometimes an egg will not be released;
- The egg and sperm may fail to meet and fertilise.
- Many early embryos fail to implant and sometimes an implanted embryo fails to develop or is rejected by the mother's body.
- An abnormality in the foetus or a lack of sufficient levels of the hormone progesterone may make it impossible for the embryo to survive, resulting in a miscarriage.

Roughly 30 per cent of infertility is caused by a problem in the woman; 30 per cent in the man; 30 per cent by both and about 10 per cent is unexplained. These figures are repeated in almost every guide to the subject, yet in reality, the figures may be somewhat different. A recent survey at the Bristol Maternity Hospital showed the main causes of infertility to be ovulatory failure (21 per cent), tubal damage (14 per cent), and sperm defects (24 per cent); 28 per cent had unexplained infertility. Unexplained infertility has tended to fall with better diagnosis and an improved understanding of what causes infertility, but is still more common than many doctors like to admit.

CAUSES OF INFERTILITY IN WOMEN

Any woman who fears that she is infertile and yet wants a child, should first see her doctor. The problem may be easily diagnosed and treatment begun without any delay. Some treatments are quite simple; for example, if the woman is not ovulating, a course of fertility drugs can be given to see if these will activate her ovaries. There are several fertility drugs, and while the doctor may know which is the best to try, often he simply has to go through each in turn, trying different doses, to see what is successful or not. This can have the effect of making the woman feel like a human guinea pig.

VISITING A FERTILITY CLINIC

If they eventually visit a fertility clinic, both partners will be asked for details of their medical history: any past illnesses and any surgery. They will also be asked questions about their sex life; how many sexual partners they have had, how often they make love, and so on. Many people find this an intrusion into their privacy, but it is all very relevant.

A routine physical examination will then be carried out on

both partners. They will be examined to check that their res-
pective reproductive organs are normal. For the man, this
means inspecting the external genitals and in particular the
testicles for any signs of a varicocele or other abnormality. The
woman will have an internal pelvic examination, during which
the doctor will insert a speculum to hold the walls of the vagina
apart so that he can view the cervix and take swabs for testing
if he suspects a vaginal infection. He will also use his hands to
feel the internal organs; this may enable him to detect problems
such as fibroids, ovarian cysts or scarring from previous
infections.

Tests undergone by the woman

One of the first tests for infertility is to find out whether the
woman is ovulating, using basal body temperature charts. At
the time of ovulation there is a small but distinct rise in the
body's temperature, due to production of the hormone progesterone. This can be measured by taking a woman's temperature every morning on waking up, a procedure which
many find irksome. A three-monthly record should show if you
are ovulating and if your cycle is normal, though you may be
asked to continue keeping a temperature chart for much longer
than this. Because temperature charts are sometimes difficult
to interpret and are not always reliable, the woman will
probably be given further tests to measure the level of
hormones which control ovulation. A blood progesterone test,
which is a simple and painless way of measuring the level of
progesterone when it reaches its peak at about day 24 in a 28
day cycle, can be done. If the level of progesterone is high, it
is a good indication that ovulation has occurred.

THE POST-COITAL TEST may also pinpoint why a
woman is not conceiving. The woman makes an appointment for the time of the month when she thinks she will
be ovulating. The couple are asked to have sexual
intercourse on the night before or the morning of the
appointment. At the clinic, the doctor will take a sample
of the woman's cervical mucus from the neck of the
womb, for examination. The quality of the mucus – clear

and slippery, or sticky and opaque – will tend to indicate whether the woman has ovulated. By examining the mucus under a microscope, it is also possible to tell if the sperm are normal, if there are enough of them and whether there are any antibodies against them. If post-coital tests are repeatedly not very good, the next step may be to test the semen and mucus for antibodies to sperm which may interfere with sperm motility.

ENDOMETRIAL BIOPSY This other procedure for assessing the woman's hormone levels involves taking a small sample of the lining of the womb for examination. This is a minor surgical procedure, similar to a D and C. The test should show if the womb lining is sufficiently primed by hormones to be able to receive the egg for implantation. If the woman is ovulating normally, the next line of investigation will be to see if the Fallopian tubes are clear.

A HYSTEROSALPINGRAM is an X-ray of the uterus and Fallopian tubes, for which purpose a dye is injected through the cervix and into the uterus. The dye passes through the womb, along the Fallopian tubes and into the pelvic cavity, enabling all the organs to be viewed. Some women may have a simpler test in which carbon dioxide gas is blown through the tubes to check if they are open; if so, the gas will enter the abdominal cavity, causing a pain under the shoulder blades, which fortunately soon wears off.

A LAPAROSCOPY is used to detect blocked or damaged tubes and other abnormalities of the womb or ovaries. Under general anaesthetic, a small incision is made in the navel and a laparoscope – a telescope-like instrument – is inserted which allows the surgeon to examine the organs in detail and assess the extent of any damage.

Tests undergone by the man

The man will be asked to produce one or more sperm samples, and this should be done at the outset, before the woman undergoes any major procedures. The man is asked to produce a sample by masturbation into a sterile container either in the clinic, or at home. If he does this at home, he must deliver the sample to the clinic within one-and-a-half hours. The sample is examined to see if the sperm are healthy, numerous and motile. Since one test is not always reliable, a poor result may mean he has to repeat the test. Sometimes a man is diagnosed as subfertile on the basis of one test alone. Yet a single sperm count is very unreliable as an indicator of a man's normal fertility. Sperm counts vary enormously from one act of intercourse to another. If all is well, this may be the only test the man has to undergo. If he has a very low or absent sperm count, however, investigations may be undertaken to see if a cause can be found. The sperm may also be examined by the post-coital test, which may give some insight into why the sperm are not functioning properly.

SCROTOTOMY
In some cases the man may have a scrototomy, an operation carried out under general anaesthetic to open up the scrotum and see whether there are any abnormalities or obstructions.

Aftermath of contraception

Contraceptive methods are a cause of infertility only very rarely. The inter-uterine device (IUD) can increase a woman's chance of suffering from pelvic inflammatory disease, which can lead to infertility. The contraceptive Pill sometimes leads to a condition called post-Pill amenorrhoea, in which a woman's periods do not return when she stops the Pill – research has shown that this only lasts for a maximum of two years after Pill use, and it can also be treated with drugs.

A woman used to taking the Pill for several years, or using an IUD or cap regularly and worrying every time her period is late, may well expect to get pregnant as soon as she stops using her chosen contraception – but often does not. This does not necessarily mean that she is infertile. However, as a woman gets older her fertility declines, and using contraception for years may mean she is less fertile when she stops and tries to get pregnant. Also, using contraception, and particularly the Pill, can disguise infertility problems for years; the Pill usually means that a woman has a regular cycle and so may not realise she is not capable of ovulating.

Hormonal problems

One of the most common causes of infertility in women is a malfunctioning of the complex hormonal interactions which govern a woman's menstrual cycle. The woman's monthly cycle is controlled by the pituitary gland in the brain which, in turn, is governed by another gland called the hypothalamus. The pituitary produces a follicle-stimulating hormone (FSH), which controls the production of the hormone oestrogen by the ovary. It also prepares one of the follicles inside the ovary to release the egg. A second pituitary hormone, luteinising hormone (LH), enables the ovary to release its egg. Oestrogen causes the lining of the womb to thicken in readiness to receive the fertilised egg.

If the egg is not fertilised, the corpus luteum begins to shrink, levels of oestrogen and progesterone decrease, the lining of the womb disintegrates and menstrual bleeding results. The falling levels of oestrogen and progesterone stimulate the pituitary to produce more FSH, and the cycle begins again.

If the egg is fertilised, however, and implants into the womb, the corpus luteum continues to produce oestrogen and progesterone until the placenta attaching the foetus to the wall of the womb is mature enough to produce the necessary hormones itself.

Failure to ovulate is normally caused by the woman's body failing to produce enough of the pituitary hormones, or releasing them at the wrong time. Since the pituitary is ultimately controlled by the hypothalamus, anything which affects the hypothalamus can also affect this gland. The hypothalamus can be affected by severe physical and emotional stress, as many women will know when the stress of travel, work, illness or emotional turmoil disrupts their menstrual cycle.

TREATMENT
Help for women unable to ovulate has been available for

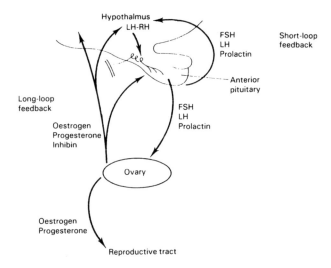

The hormonal interactions which govern the menstrual cycle.

many years in the form of fertility drugs. There are two main types: those which prod the pituitary into producing FSH and LH on time and those which replace FSH and LH if this approach fails:

• **Clomiphene (Clomid)** is an artificial drug which triggers the release of FSH and LH in the pituitary. It seems to induce ovulation in about 80 per cent of women treated, though not all these will succeed in getting pregnant. One reason for this is that clomiphene tends to prevent the cervical mucus from becoming fluid at the fertile time in the month to enable the sperm to enter the womb. This problem can sometimes be overcome by giving oestrogen as well in the few days before ovulation.

Sometimes a combination of clomiphene and human chorionic gonadotrophin (HCG, a hormone produced by the young embryo) given on the fourteenth day of the cycle will induce women to ovulate who would not do so on clomiphene alone.

Clomiphene also seems to help women with a progesterone deficiency.

Clomiphene (Clomid) has been in use for many years
and is considered safe, although a few women do have
unpleasant side-effects, such as nausea, feeling bloated, or
very rarely, enlargement of the ovaries accompanied by
pain in the pelvis. Some infertility specialists deny the
severity of these symptoms, or fail to inform women of
them.

Recently there has been some concern that clomiphene
might cause an increase in the number of eggs released
following its use which have chromosomal abnormalities.
Others have questioned whether there might be other
long-term effects on the children who are conceived after
their mothers took fertility drugs, as happened with
women who took the drug DES (diethylstilboestrel) in
early pregnancy to prevent a miscarriage. This is of
particular concern to women who take large doses of
fertility drugs to make them produce more than one egg,
or superovulate, as is done for IVF and other treatments.
However, there is no evidence to support such fears as yet.

• **Human menopausal gonadotrophin, (HMG), or
Pergonal**, is a hormone extracted from the urine of
pregnant women and prepares the follicles which release
the egg to ripen. It is usually given with an injection of
another drug, HCG, which actually triggers ovulation.
About 90 per cent of women will ovulate with this
treatment, though again not all will conceive and some
will miscarry. About 20 to 30 per cent of pregnancies
resulting from this treatment will be twins or more; HMG
is responsible for most of the multiple pregnancies which
occur with fertility drugs.

The hormone HMG is very potent and may also over-
stimulate the ovaries, so its level in the blood and urine
needs to be monitored daily. A new development which
might overcome this problem is a small 'pump' about the
size of a pocket book which, attached to the woman's arm,
provides small, even doses of hormone through a fine
needle. However, having a pump attached day and night

and having to go and have the needle repositioned when necessary can be unpleasant.

For women who do not ovulate with either of these drugs, there may be hope with a drug called bromocriptine. Some women do not ovulate because they have in their blood a high level of a hormone called prolactin, which is normally only produced in quantity while women are breastfeeding and tends to prevent ovulation. Bromocriptine prevents the pituitary from producing prolactin, and after treatment with it ovulation occurs in about 95 per cent of women who previously produced too much prolactin.

Scarring or structural abnormalities

The other major causes of infertility in women are scarring of the reproductive organs by past disease or surgery, or structural abnormalities present from birth.

- Untreated sexually transmitted diseases, especially gonorrhoea, can result in infertility. As many as 80 per cent of infected women never have any severe symptoms with the disease, and may not realise that they have it and infection has spread to the Fallopian tubes, causing damage.
- PID (pelvic inflammatory disease) which can start after an induced abortion or miscarriage, after childbirth, after surgery in the pelvic region or after infection with a sexually transmitted disease, can cause tubal scarring and blockage.
- Other infections which can affect fertility are chlamydia and mycoplasmas. Chlamydia, a bacterium which closely resembles a large virus, has deceptively mild symptoms and an untreated 'silent' infection can destroy the inside of a woman's Fallopian tubes in a matter of days. Mycoplasmas, another organism, may affect fertility and has been held responsible for miscarriages.

Other Causes

Endometriosis is a disease which may affect as many as five to ten per cent of women at some stage in their reproductive lives. The condition is caused by patches of the endometrial tissue which lines the womb, or endometrium, becoming deposited outside the womb. This tissue, like the womb lining, thickens and bleeds with each menstrual cycle. Scar tissue is then formed which may block the ends of the Fallopian tubes, or adhesions may form which prevent the tube from picking up the egg on its release from the ovary.

Endometriosis can be treated by a number of drugs; birth control pills or progesterone, or a drug called Danazol, which blocks production of the two pituitary hormones. The idea is that these treatments 'switch off' the menstrual cycle, stopping the patches of endometrial tissue from bleeding; they will then fade away, and any adhesions or scar tissue can be removed by careful surgery.

FIBROIDS OR POLYPS IN THE WOMB are benign growths which can affect fertility by growing to a size large enough to cause blockage or prevent the egg implanting and growing. These can be removed by surgery.

MALFORMATIONS OF THE WOMB, such as the presence of a dividing wall or septum, again can sometimes be corrected by surgery.

• A further cause of damage to the tubes is previous surgery in the abdominal region. Bleeding or trauma to the tissues may result in the formation of scar tissue or adhesions which may then block or fix the tubes, ovaries or womb into unnatural positions that make it impossible for the egg to pass from the ovaries into the Fallopian tubes, making conception impossible. One leading British microsurgeon who has specialised in repairing damaged Fallopian tubes has criticized surgeons for not taking enough care when operating in the abdominal region of women of childbearing age. Of 108 women with tubal damage referred to the Hammersmith Hospital, London over a three-month period, 73 per cent had had previous pelvic surgery.

Increasing skill in carrying out delicate microsurgery has given more women with blocked Fallopian tubes a chance to achieve pregnancy. However, if surgery is not effective, there is still hope through the test-tube baby treatment or IVF (see Chapter 4).

TUBAL OR ECTOPIC PREGNANCY

Occasionally a fertilised egg fails to move down through the tube and into the womb and, instead, grows in the tube. Eventually it will burst the tube, causing considerable bleeding and damage.

An ectopic pregnancy thus results in both the loss of one pregnancy and a possible barrier to future conception. One tube is almost inevitably lost and the other may be damaged by bleeding caused by the tube rupturing or surgery to remove the pregnancy. It is estimated that about fifty per cent of women who have an ectopic pregnancy may never conceive again.

Often an ectopic pregnancy occurs when there has been some damage to the tube, perhaps caused by past infections or surgery. It is also more common if a woman becomes pregnant with an IUD in place. An ectopic pregnancy is very painful and can be life-threatening. However, prompt medical attention to remove the developing egg before the tube can burst avoids many risks as well as improving the chances of successfully reconstructing the damaged tube.

Multiple early miscarriage

This is another problem which is now being recognised as a cause of infertility. Some women are able to produce eggs that are fertilised and even begin to implant into the lining of the womb, but then fail to develop further, resulting in an early miscarriage. At one time most women to whom this happened probably did not ever realise that they had conceived. With early, sensitive pregnancy tests that allow a woman to know she has conceived even before her period is late, many more women are realising that they have suffered an early pregnancy loss.

Miscarriages are very common – about one in seven pregnancies are estimated to end in miscarriage, and the figure would probably be even higher if all early pregnancy losses were detected and included. About half of them are caused by abnormalities in the foetus that prevent further growth. Miscarriages are more common in first pregnancies and some doctors think that these pregnancies are a kind of 'trial run'. The risk of miscarriage increases with age, and miscarriages following fertility treatment are also more common than in other women.

Most women who suffer one or even two miscarriages go on to have a normal pregnancy. Only after three successive miscarriages do the risks of having another go up substantially. Some women however have repeated miscarriages, and seem unable to carry a baby to term. Sometimes this happens because the woman or her partner are carrying a chromosomal abnormality. It has recently been recognised, however, that some women miscarry because they are rejecting the baby in their womb as foreign. In a normal pregnancy, the woman's immune system is activated in such a way that she does not recognise the baby as a foreign body and reject it. Some women and their partners seem to be a poor genetic match, so that partner's baby will always be rejected. Immunising the woman with an injection of her partner's white blood cells can overcome this rejection problem and allow her to have a normal pregnancy and baby.

INFERTILITY IN MEN

Male infertility can also be caused by blocked tubes, the vasa deferentia, which carry sperm from the testes where they are made to the penis. Tubes can be blocked for any of the following reasons:

- From birth due to a congenital defect.
- Through scarring caused by sexually transmitted diseases.
- Through surgery, as in a vasectomy.

Male infertility can also be caused by:

- Undescended testicles – if these are not diagnosed early in a boy's life permanent infertility will result.
- By infections involving the testicles; orchitis, inflammation of the testicles following mumps, very occasionally can result in infertility.
- Varicocele – a sort of varicose vein of the testicle – is a common cause of male infertility.

- Rarely, disorders of ejaculation are responsible for male infertility. Sometimes, as a result of illness such as diabetes or surgery such as a prostatectomy, sperm is ejaculated backwards into the bladder at orgasm.
- Male infertility is also the result of a low sperm count, or of a large proportion of the man's sperm being abnormal. Although research is being done, no-one really understands the causes of low sperm counts; however, their origin is believed to be hormonal.

TREATMENTS

Because so little is understood about the causes of much male infertility, very limited help is available for the majority of men with a low or absent sperm count. Some causes are known (see above) but there is little to be done about them.

The most curable form of male infertility is that caused by a varicocele, or varicose vein, around the testicle. A simple operation to tie off the vein results in an improvement to sperm quantity and quality in about two-thirds of cases, thus increasing the chances of conception.

Blocked or scarred vasa deferentia, especially after vasectomy, may be restored surgically but there is only a 50 per cent success rate; this is because a man with blocked tubes often produces antibodies to the sperm as they cannot be ejaculated and have to be reabsorbed by the body.

Other causes of a low sperm count are very resistant to treatment. Various hormone treatments have been tried, but with a very low success rate. Some studies have shown that the success rate is actually lower among treated men than among those who have not received any drugs at all. Many of the drugs – some of which are the same as female fertility drugs – also have unpleasant side-effects such as loss of libido, swollen breasts or loss of body hair. To a man whose self-esteem is already dented by the fact of his infertility, these side-effects can be impossible to bear.

One new technique that may help men with a low sperm count, is the split ejaculate technique, where the first part of several ejaculates – the part richest in sperm – is pooled and introduced into the vagina through artificial insemination. This may not work, however, where a large number of abnormal sperm are present.

Now IVF and similar techniques such as GIFT offer new hope for subfertile men (see Chapter 4 for full details). Far fewer sperm are needed to achieve fertilisation in vitro, as the sperm do not have to make their arduous journey through the vagina, cervix, womb and tubes, with most being left behind at one stage or another.

Sometimes sperm are capable of fertilising an egg but not of penetrating the cervix or surviving long in the woman's reproductive tract. By mixing sperm directly with the egg, as in IVF, these problems may be overcome.

SELF-HELP

Some men can improve sperm counts with a healthier diet, stopping or reducing smoking and drinking alcohol, avoiding hot baths and not wearing tight underwear.

Since the testes are very sensitive to heat, men who work in a very hot environment sometimes experience a reduction in fertility; this can also sometimes be avoided.

Sperm counts can also be lowered by illness, especially involving a fever; sperm counts can be reduced for some time afterwards since it takes three months for sperm to be produced in the body. Fortunately, this is a short-term problem that will resolve itself.

OTHER POSSIBLE TREATMENTS

If the measures described in this chapter fail, or if the sperm count is consistently so low that conception is very unlikely, the main alternative is artificial insemination by donor (AID) (see Chapter 4).

Going through the tests and treatments already described is in itself a remarkable testament to most couple's desire for a child they can call their own. By the time these couples come to consider assisted reproduction techniques, they have probably already been through months or years of tests and the more orthodox fertility treatments. At the same time, it can be difficult to call a halt.

'You feel you've already invested so many years and so much pain in all this, you just have to go on to the end,' said one woman.

3

Facing up to infertility

Infertility is a difficult problem because many people feel that they are personally responsible for it. Having had an abortion in the past, delaying having a baby till later in life, using a method of contraception which may have affected fertility, can all haunt the infertile.

If infertility is unexplained – as about 10 per cent of it is – the couple may wonder if there is a psychological element. Couples are told to 'Relax, then you will conceive.' Some doctors and psychiatrists do believe that stress and anxiety can block conception.

One biochemist, Paul Entwhistle at Liverpool University, claims that 65 per cent of around 200 patients who had tried conventional infertility treatments conceived after hypno-therapy. He believes that a woman may 'switch off' her fertility subconsciously, failing to ovulate or making her tubes go into spasm, or affecting the blood supply in her womb, and so preventing implantation. This may explain why some women conceive after a dramatic event like moving home, starting a new job, or adopting a child, and why the chances of getting pregnant after a single act of rape seem higher than after a single act of sex in a consenting relationship – the shock may prevent the woman 'switching off' her fertility.

Obviously the mind and body are closely linked, and depression and anxiety clearly do have effects on fertility. A loss of interest in sex causes drying up of the vaginal secretions that help sperm motility; it also reduces rates of sexual intercourse.

However, most psychological explanations of infertility concentrate on the woman; I have never seen a single suggestion that anxiety, stress or deep-seated fear of fatherhood might cause a man to have a low sperm count. The fact that people, especially women, often blame themselves for their infertility may make the stress of infertility far worse for them. Being considered to be neurotic or psychologically unstable – and even partially responsible for their condition – does not help a couple who want to have a child and seek treatment to realise that aim.

Infertility can also isolate people: from friends or contemporaries with children, and even from their families who may not understand. One infertile woman remembers the pain of hearing her mother say that she would have to advertise for some grandchildren; she was clearly hurt by her daughter's infertility but could not share the pain with her. Others find that friends and neighbours assume that they have chosen to be childless. Some are told they are 'lucky' to be childless or that they should 'make the best of it'. Infertility is little understood and is considered embarrassing to many because it implies sexual inadequacy of some kind. It often turns people in on themselves because they feel they cannot share their pain with others.

SOME REACTIONS TO INFERTILITY

Whatever the cause of infertility, the dawning realisation that having a baby may be difficult or impossible is very traumatic for most people. Infertility is one of the worst experiences many people have to cope with in their whole lives. Those who discover that they are infertile speak of it as a terrible blow, as bad for some as receiving the news that they are to lose part of their body or have a potentially terminal illness. One woman shows this clearly, when she recalls the feelings she had on receiving her diagnosis: 'They told me not only that I couldn't have children but that I had cancer. The first thing that struck me was grief that I couldn't have a baby. The fact that I also had cancer hit me about 30 seconds later.'

In Robert and Elizabeth Snowden's book, *The Gift of a Child*, a husband described his reactions on being told he was infertile. 'Anyone who's never actually been told, you can't tell them the feeling that you get. It's like being hit with a sledge-hammer . . . I never felt so ill in my life. It took me a long while to get over it.'

With men in particular, the discovery of infertility can trigger problems with sexuality. One American doctor who studied the reactions of men recently informed of their infertility found that almost two-thirds suffered a period of impotence lasting one to three months after hearing this news.

Anger, resentment and guilt

Jenny Hunt, an infertility counsellor at the Hammersmith Hospital, London, says that many couples have what might seem quite extreme reactions to the discovery of infertility. Many experience a loss of self-image, and may even hate themselves. They may hate their bodies, and in particular their genitals, which they feel are useless and have betrayed them.

One woman said that she hated her body, it seemed so ugly and useless. 'I remember saying to the consultant, well that's it then, I might as well have a double mastectomy and a hyster-ectomy now. What use is my womb and what use are my breasts if I will never use them to carry or feed a baby? He didn't understand me at all. He just seemed very shocked at my response.'

Such reactions may sound excessive, but they are not unusual. Many infertile people have self-mutilating fantasies, due to the anger they feel towards their bodies for letting them down.

Sometimes one partner feels anger at the other one for being infertile. Jenny Hunt says that most wives of infertile husbands feel angry with them and hate themselves for it. Others, male and female, feel that if they are the one responsible for the infertility problem, their partner should feel free to divorce them and find someone else. 'If I can't have (or give you) children, feel free to go and find someone who can,' is the common cry.

Depression and grief

Many infertile couples need help in working through their very understandable emotions. Many of the problems can be overcome when a couple have genuinely accepted their infertility, or have found ways around it. But at the time, this may seem impossible. Depression may set in and occasionally an infertile woman turns her depression inwards and attempts suicide. For such women, having a baby has become more important even than life itself.

The grief felt by infertile couples is of a very particular kind. Unlike the loss of a parent, relative, child or loved one, when a couple are infertile they grieve the loss of a person they have never known. Normally when a person grieves they have memories to treasure and to comfort them, but an infertile couple have only lost hopes and fantasies. Even so, they go through all the usual phases of grief – denial, anger, mourning, acceptance. Because with many forms of infertility there is always a small hope that the couple will succeed, some people get stuck somewhere in the grieving process. Others have their hopes awoken again, and this makes it much more difficult to accept a final 'negative' diagnosis.

As one mother said, 'People were always trotting out to me stories of women who had finally conceived after years and years of waiting. "Oh, so-and-so, down the road, she had to wait six years and then she had this beautiful baby boy." Or, "What about this test-tube baby thing, have you tried that?" They are always trying to give you hope when you know you should give up. I used to cling to every story I heard about people having babies against innumerable odds, as I so much wanted to believe that there was hope. It made adjusting to the whole problem so much harder.'